C. S. Lewis
Journal

C. S. Lewis Journal

eagle
Guildford, Surrey

This compilation has been made possible thanks to Kathryn Lindskoog and Susan Wavre. The daily quotes from Kathryn Lindskoog's book *Around the Year with C. S. Lewis and his Friends*, published by The C. R. Gibson Company, Norwalk, Connecticut 06856, have been selected, condensed and re-arranged for the purposes of this book by Susan Wavre. She has also selected, principally from the original sources, the quotes from C. S. Lewis himself, which feature at the close of each week.

British Library Cataloguing in Publication Data. A catalogue record for this book is available from the British Library.

Published by Eagle, an imprint of Inter Publishing Service (IPS) Ltd, St Nicholas House, 14 The Mount, Guildford, Surrey GU2 5HN.

Typeset by Eagle
Printed in Singapore
ISBN No: 0 86347 192 7

This journal belongs to:

....

Introduction

C. S. Lewis was undoubtedly the greatest Christian writer, communicator and apologist of this century. His output was always diverse and original. He made a name as a significant writer of adult science fiction with books such as *Out of the Silent Planet*. His fantasy books aimed at children, the Narnia Chronicles, have been read by tens of millions worldwide – often without them realising the extent of the Christian imagery they contain. Countless others have been sustained and inspired by the the deeper meaning of Aslan's all-conquering victory over the White Witch and the massed forces of darkness.

To others, Lewis was primarily the author of a surprising range of well-argued, insightful Christian books which helped them on their spiritual journey. For many, reading *Mere Christianity* was in fact the starting point of that journey.

And yet his books of Christian apologetics happened rather accidently: it must not be forgotten that it was a selection of his highly successful wartime BBC radio broadcasts collated into book form by popular demand which popularised his Christian writing career. C. S. Lewis was first and foremost an Oxford don – a university professor of English literature and language.

As a student Lewis had quickly acquired three first class degrees; Greek and Latin; philosophy; and finally English language and literature specialising in Old English. Then in 1925 he applied for, and was given, an English fellowship at Magdalen College, Oxford. This brought him a secure teaching post, rooms in college, a generous income and the freedom to indulge in his main areas of interest: Anglo Saxon and Norse myths and medieval allegory.

This interest was to find its practical application many years later in his writing, both specifically Christian and more obviously in the Narnia Chronicles. In fact his first book, now widely ignored was an allegory, *The Pilgrim's Regress*, published in 1933 two years after his conversion and which traces a spiritual journey. It opens with the hero John experiencing as a boy the law as institutional religion represented it. But his next experience, which feels like an emotional explosion, is a vision of a far-off island, and a tremendous longing for it. It is this longing or desire that sets him off on his journey, much of which is spent in meeting people who either dismiss this longing and its object, or suggest false paths towards it.

These themes of longing, desire and of journeying can be found in most of Lewis' subsequent work, and are in fact intrinsic to our experience as humans made in the image of God, journeying on this earth. A very real way for each of us to journey is to do so in reading with a gentle and wise guide, accompanied and surrounded by friends. The guide here is C. S. Lewis himself, as experiences and events from his life have been carefully selected and presented along with quotes from his books and his many friends – some from among the Inklings, a group of Oxford academics with an interest in fantasy – his brother Warren, and many others who he was influenced by, or who he himself influenced.

This journal enables the reader to join C. S. Lewis in that journey. Each week starts with entries recalling significant events in C. S. Lewis' life, or that of someone close to him, that happened during that week: books published, articles written, broadcasts and lectures delivered, friendships, joys and tears, and most importantly, his significant spiritual milestones are noted. The reader is then left with sufficient space within which to journal before a concluding quote from C. S. Lewis, a friend or one of his favourite authors completes the week.

Week 1

JANUARY 1ST~ 7TH

Jan 3rd - 1892, J. R. Tolkien's birthday.
Jan 3rd - 1945, Jill Flewett, a 17-year-old who had, like many others, been sent to the country from London to be safe from the bombing during the Second World War, left the Lewis home to return to London. She remained a lifelong friend of the Lewis brothers.
Jan 6th - 1939, Warren and C. S. Lewis completed their last annual walking tour across open countryside.

Living with Lewis was like having one's own private tutor . . . the whole of my time there he built up my confidence in myself and in my ability to think . . . I left the Kilns with deeper and more understanding, and with a belief that I was of value.

Jill Flewett Freud, in the *Canadian C. S. Lewis Journal*

Week 2

January 8th–14th

Jan 10th ~ 1950, C. S. Lewis received a letter from Joy Davidman Gresham of the United States. She was turning to him for counsel after his books had led her to Christianity. This contact eventually led to their marriage.

Jan 11th ~ 1923, C. S. Lewis read George MacDonald's *Phantastes* at tea, noting that he had read it many times and that it filled the place of a devotional book for him.

Jan 13th ~ 1919, C. S. Lewis arrived in Oxford to take the Honour Mods course in Greek and Latin literature.

I never had been by any means a book-worm; but the very outside of a book had a charm to me. It was a kind of sacrament – an outward and visible sign of an inward and spiritual grace as, indeed, what on God's earth is not?

George MacDonald, *The Portent*

Week 3

January 15th~21st

Jan 19th ~ 1932, Warren Lewis received an important letter from C. S. Lewis, in which he admitted he had started to go to Communion; this meant he had become a Christian. So had Warren.

Jan 21st ~ 1955, C. S. Lewis published an essay called 'Prudery and Philology' in the *Spectator.*

In God there is no hunger that needs to be filled, only plenteousness that desires to give.

C. S. Lewis, *The Four Loves*

Week 4

January 22nd-28th

Jan 23rd - 1954, C. S. Lewis wrote a letter to his ex-student and friend, Dom Bede Griffiths, saying that Dickens and Tolstoy were two of his favourite authors, both great writers about affection.

Jan 24th - 1954, C. S. Lewis lunched with Joy Davidman Gresham (his future wife) and Ruth Pitter (winner of the Queen's Medal for poetry).

Jan 26th - 1942, the first official meeting of the Socratic Club took place in Oxford. At this club, sponsored by C. S. Lewis, he often defended the Christian faith in lively debates.

I would say that the secret of his power and his life was the depth of his own devotion to our Lord.

Stella Aldwinkle, founder of the Socratic Club, on a BBC Radio programme about C. S. Lewis in 1978

Week 5

JAN 29TH–FEB 4TH

Feb 1st - 1918, apparent misfortune was really good fortune when C. S. Lewis was hospitalised with trench fever; in the hospital he rested and first read the writing of G. K. Chesterton.

Feb 2nd - 1942, C. S. Lewis was defeated by Elizabeth Anscombe, professor of philosophy, in an informal debate in the Socratic Club. It was Lewis' only recorded defeat in any public forum in his entire life, and he made a small revision in his book *Miracles* because of Anscombe's point.

Feb 4th - 1933, C. S. Lewis wrote to his friend Arthur Greeves expressing his delight in a children's story just written by his new friend J. R R. Tolkien. It would be published in 1937 as *The Hobbit*.

I am as susceptible as a dragon to flattery.

J. R.R. Tolkien, in *The Observer*

Week 6

Feb 5th-11th

Feb 8th - 1951, C. S. Lewis was defeated for the Poetry Chair at Oxford.
Feb 10th - 1938, C. S. Lewis' poem 'The Future of Forestry', which expressed his great love for trees, was published in *Oxford Magazine*.
Feb 11th - 1923, C. S. Lewis took his first walk with his new friend Nevill Coghill. He soon had the shock of discovering that Coghill, the most intelligent and best-informed man in their class, was a believing Christian.

If you are on the wrong road, progress means doing an about-turn and walking back to the right road.

C. S. Lewis, *Mere Christianity*

Week 7

Feb 12th~18th

Feb 12th - 1918, C. S. Lewis wrote to his friend Arthur Greeves from a British Red Cross hospital in France, remarking about how much he was still enjoying Boswell's *Life of Dr Johnson.*
Feb 13th - 1960, C. S. Lewis wrote to an American correspondent expressing hopes for a trip to Greece. He said it would mean much to him and his wife Joy to have stood once on the Acropolis in Athens.
Feb 18th - 1938, J. R. R. Tolkien wrote to his editor Stanley Unwin recommending C. S. Lewis' manuscript *Out of the Silent Planet.*

If a man does not make new acquaintances as he advances through life, he will soon find himself left alone. A man, sir, should keep his friendships in a constant repair.

Samuel Johnson, in Boswell's *Life of Dr Johnson*

Week 8

FEB 19TH~25TH

Feb 19th ~ 1955, C. S. Lewis pointed out to one of his many correspondents that by coincidence he was transferring from Magdalen College, Oxford, to Magdalene College, Cambridge. Both are pronounced Maudlin, and both are named after Mary Magdalene.

Feb 21st ~ 1945, C. S. Lewis published his article on evolution and creation, 'Who Was Right – Dream Lecturer or Real Lecturer?' in the *Coventry Evening Telegraph.*

Feb 23rd ~ 1959, C. S. Lewis spoke on Samuel Pepys at the annual Pepys dinner in Cambridge, held on Pepys' birthday (1633).

Feb 24th ~ 1943, C. S. Lewis began his Riddel Memorial Lectures on the Abolition of Man, in Durham.

Such different birds are hatched from the same nest.

George MacDonald, *Sir Gibbie*

Week 9

Feb 26th–March 4th

Feb 26th - 1936, C. S. Lewis reported reading his first book by Charles Williams, *The Place of the Lion.*
Feb 27th - 1948, C. S. Lewis recorded his preface to *The Great Divorce* for BBC Radio.
Feb 29th - 1952, C. S. Lewis sent his 'condolences and congratulations' to a woman who had recently become a Christian. He told her that an adult conversion usually has some difficulties, like learning to swim or getting married or taking up a profession.
March 1st - 1918, C. S. Lewis returned bravely to the front lines in France after his bout of trench fever.

In reading Chesterton, as in reading MacDonald, I did not know what I was letting myself in for. A young man who wishes to remain a sound Atheist cannot be too careful of his reading.

C. S. Lewis, *Surprised by Joy*

Week 10

March 5th~11th

March 5th - 1908, C. S. Lewis, aged nine, completed his first reading of Milton's *Paradise Lost.*
March 11th - 1936, C. S. Lewis wrote to Charles Williams for the first time.

Lewis, with the gusto of a Chesterton or a Belloc, would suddenly roar out a passage of poetry that he had newly discovered and memorized.

Nevill Coghill in *Light on C. S. Lewis*

Week 11

March 12th~18th

March 12th - 1919, C. S. Lewis delivered his first paper, on William Morris, to the Martlets Society, a select literary group at Oxford, of which Lewis was elected secretary in January of this year.
March 14th - 1921, C. S. Lewis visited, for the first time, William Butler Yeats – who had long been established as the foremost poet of Ireland and who in 1924 was to receive the Nobel Prize.

C. S. Lewis said during my 1963 interview with him, 'There are many different ways of bringing people into God's kingdom, even some ways that I specially dislike. I have therefore learned to be cautious'.

Sherwood Wirt, *Freshness of the Spirit*

Week 12

March 19th~25th

March 25th - 1931, Warren Lewis wrote to some stained-glass makers to arrange for them to make a church window, that he and C. S. Lewis had planned together in honour of their parents, for the church in Belfast where their grandfather had once been the preacher and their parents had attended.

The perfect church service would be one we were almost unaware of; our attention would have been on God.

C. S. Lewis, *Letters to Malcolm*

Week 13

March 26th~April 1st

March 26th ~ 1947, C. S. Lewis met with two archbishops and the Marquis of Salisbury at Lambeth Palace to discuss the future of the Church of England.
March 31st ~ 1946, C. S. Lewis preached at his local church.

C. S. Lewis as a child, c 1907. c Bodleian Library.

Brasenose College built in 1509, seen through a gateway in Radcliffe Square.

The library, chapel and gardens of Exeter College. (opposite)

Most of Hertford College, including the well-known 'Bridge of Sighs' was built around 1820.

The inner Quad of Jesus College is one of the best preserved medieval quads.

The tower of Magdalen College Chapel, completed in 1509, seen from the Botanical Gardens.

The rose garden at Magdalen College, with some of the original buildings dating from 1474 in the background.

C.S. Lewis: a characteristic pose. c Hulton Picture Library.

It is the heart that is not yet sure of its God that is afraid to laugh in His presence.

George MacDonald, *Sir Gibbie*

Week 14

April 2nd~8th

April 2nd ~ 1922, C. S. Lewis sat by an open window and began writing his book-length poem *Dymer*. It began with Dymer rebelling in April.

April 3rd ~ 1960, C. S. Lewis and his wife Joy flew from London to Athens with their friends Roger Lancelyn Green and his wife June.

April 4th ~ 1945, C. S. Lewis published 'The Laws of Nature' in the *Coventry Evening Telegraph*.

April 6th ~ 1960, C. S. Lewis visited Daphne, Greece, with his wife Joy. Later he said that it was among the supreme days of his life.

'There is no bond like the bond of having read and liked the same books,' says someone in one of E. Nesbit's stories: and that was how I got to know C. S. Lewis.

Roger Lancelyn Green, 'C. S. Lewis', in *Puffin Annual Number One*

Week 15

April 9th~15th

April 13th ~ 1944, C. S. Lewis, J. R. R. Tolkien, Charles Williams and R. E. Havard listened to Warren Lewis read a chapter of his first book, *The Splendid Century*, on this evening.

April 14th ~ 1960, C. S. Lewis returned with his wife Joy to England after their tour of Greece.

April 15th ~ 1947, Warren and C. S. Lewis ended a pleasant eleven~day vacation in Malvern. They liked to visit their friend George Sayer there.

True friendship is the least jealous of loves.

C. S. Lewis, *The Four Loves*

Week 16

April 16th~22nd

April 16th ~ 1933, C. S. Lewis got an idea on this day for a book about lost souls going on a visit to Paradise. The result was his book, *The Great Divorce*, published in 1945.
April 18th ~ 1944, C. S. Lewis spoke very briefly on Christianity and Modern Industry and then answered questions from factory workers at Electric and Musical Industries Ltd. in Hayes, Middlesex.
April 21st ~ 1905, the Lewis family moved into their newly~built, large, peculiar, inefficient house called Little Lea in the suburbs of Belfast. Warren and C. S. Lewis were eight and six years old.

C. S. Lewis was often frivolous, a great source of fun for his friends. This side of a complex personality is too often neglected.

George Sayer in a personal letter recalling C. S. Lewis

Week 17

April 23rd–29th

April 23rd - 1956, C. S. Lewis secretly married Joy Davidman in a civil ceremony to enable her to stay in England. Also Shakespeare's birthday (1564).

April 24th - 1930, Warren and C. S. Lewis said farewell to their childhood home in Belfast, Little Lea. Oxford would be their permanent home, but they would always enjoy returning to Ireland for visits.

He certainly wrote the best academic prose in our time that I've ever read.

John Wain. Professor of Poetry at Oxford, on a 1978 programme about Lewis.

Week 18

APRIL 30TH~MAY 6TH

April 30th ~ 1953, C. S. Lewis gave his last Socratic Club presentation, 'Faith and Evidence'. This essay is now called 'Obstinacy and Belief'.
May 1st ~ 1930, Warren and C. S. Lewis arose before 5 a.m. and climbed Magdalen Tower before sunrise for the festivities – a sunrise ceremony on May Day having long been traditional at Magdalen College, Oxford, where C. S. Lewis taught from 1925 to 1955.
May 6th ~ 1937, C. S. Lewis published his poem 'Coronation March' in *Oxford Magazine*.

Only those who try to resist temptation know how strong it is.

C. S. Lewis, *Mere Christianity*

Week 19

May 7th~13th

May 7th ~ 1963, C. S. Lewis was interviewed in Cambridge by Sherwood Wirt, editor of Billy Graham's *Decision* magazine.
May 8th ~ 1946, C. S. Lewis' poem 'On Being Human' was published in *Punch*. In it he contrasted the purely spiritual nature of angels with our human dependence upon our physical brains and our five senses, which make our lives so beautiful.
May 9th ~ 1945, the war in Europe ended.
May 11th ~ 1926, C. S. Lewis and J. R. R. Tolkien got acquainted for the first time.

And if we believe that God is everywhere, why should we not think Him present even in the coincidences that sometimes seem so strange? For, if He be in the things that coincide, He must be in the coincidence of those things

George MacDonald, *Annals of a Quiet Neighbourhood*

Week 20

May 14th–20th

May 14th ~ 1955, C. S. Lewis and Dorothy Sayers published their article 'Charles Williams' in *The Times.*
May 15th ~ 1955, C. S. Lewis and Dorothy Sayers initiated public tributes in London, Oxford and Cambridge, honouring Charles Williams.
May 20th ~ 1925, C. S. Lewis was offered a five-year position as tutor of English language and literature at Magdalen College, Oxford. (He was to stay in that position for thirty years.)

If you had delayed writing another 24 hours our letters would have crossed . . . It has never before happened to me to be admiring an author of a book while he at the same time was admiring me.

Charles Williams, answer to C. S. Lewis

Week 21

May 21st-27th

May 21st - 1936, C. S. Lewis published his first book about literature, *The Allegory of Love.*
May 25th - 1930, on this Sunday, Warren Lewis, stationed at Bulford army camp on Salisbury Plain, very thoughtfully decided that he would accept C. S. Lewis' invitation to join his household as soon as he was free to do so. As he seemed to know, that was a lifetime decision.
May 27th - 1926, John Betjeman, one of C. S. Lewis' earliest pupils, came to his Anglo-Saxon tutorial in eccentric bedroom slippers. In 1972, aged 66, Sir John became Poet Laureate.

In reading great literature I become a thousand men and yet remain myself.

C. S. Lewis, 'An Experiment in Criticism'

Week 22

May 28th–June 3rd

May 28th - 1945, C. S. Lewis' defence of prayer, 'Work and Prayer', appeared in the *Coventry Evening Telegraph*.
May 31st - 1951, C. S. Lewis invited his friend Roger Lancelyn Green to be the person to write his biography.
June 2nd - 1938, C. S. Lewis and J. R. R. Tolkien succeeded in getting their friend Adam Fox elected Professor of Poetry at Oxford.

. . . C. S. Lewis, remarkable perhaps most of all because he was notably detached from this world and yet made so great an impact on it.

Adam Fox, 'C. S. Lewis at the Breakfast Table'

Week 23

June 4th~June 10th

June 7th ~ C. S. Lewis once began a lecture on Sir Walter Scott by describing how, on this night in 1826, Scott, in poor health, bankrupt, and newly bereaved, was kept awake by a howling dog.
June 8th ~ 1944, Warren and C. S. Lewis, J. R. R. Tolkien, Charles Williams and E. R. Eddison (author of the fantasy *The Worm Ouroboros*) spent the evening in Lewis's room at Magdalen reading to each other.

I was glad to see them go and glad to have them back again.

Warren Lewis's thoughts about the pleasure of solitude.

Week 24

June 11th– 17th

June 11th – 1954, C. S. Lewis's poem 'Science Fiction Cradlesong' was published in the *Times Literary Supplement*; it analyses the true desire involved in space travel.

June 14th – 1923, C. S. Lewis took his school exams and he didn't know if he had done well or not.

June 16th – 1895, birth of Warren Hamilton Lewis.

June 17th – 1918, C. S. Lewis wrote triumphantly to his Irish friend Arthur Greeves describing the opera *The Valkyrie* that he had just seen at Drury Lane Theatre, London.

It's so much easier to pray for a bore than to go and see him.

C. S. Lewis, *Letters to Malcolm*

Week 25

June 18th~24th

June 19th ~ 1959, C. S. Lewis wrote to fellow literature professor Kathleen Raine to advise her to stay at Cambridge. If she stayed, he said, she could always leave later; but if she left, she couldn't come back.

June 20th ~ 1916, C. S. Lewis wrote to his writing partner and friend Arthur Greeves issuing an ultimatum. If Greeves did not send Lewis some literary efforts by midnight of the last day in June, Lewis would cut off all communication with him.

June 21st ~ 1930, C. S. Lewis moved to Headington; within weeks he would discover his future home, The Kilns, in Headington Quarry.

June 22nd ~ 1921, C. S. Lewis read portions of his Chancellor's Prize essay at the ceremony of Encaenin in the Oxford Sheldonian Theatre.

June 23rd ~ 1944, C. S. Lewis's poem '*Vitrea Circe*' was published in *Punch.* The poem retells one of the incidents in Homer's *Odyssey,* which C. S. Lewis considered the greatest novel ever written.

He [God] regards men not as they are merely, but as they shall be; not as they shall be merely, but as they are now growing.

George MacDonald, 'The Consuming Fire'

Week 26

June 25th–July 1st

June 29th - 1947, Warren Lewis was released from the Convent Hospital of Our Lady of Lourdes in Drogheda, Ireland.
July 1st - 1923, C. S. Lewis wrote to his father, thanking him heartily for his extended education and asking for even more, in hopes of becoming a don at Oxford.

I feel it would be the height of impudence on my part to suppose that what I would have found tedious to write, anyone else would have found interesting to read.

Warren Lewis's foreword to his first completed book, *The Splendid Century*, explaining why he left out dull material

Week 27

JULY 2ND~8TH

July 6th ~ 1930, Warren and C. S. Lewis saw The Kilns, their future home for the rest of their lives, for the first time. It was for sale for £3,500, and they knew this was a wonderful opportunity.
July 8th ~ 1930, C. S. Lewis wrote a long letter to his friend Arthur Greeves. He said that he could go on quoting from Traherne's meditations forever.

Do not waste time bothering whether you 'love' your neighbour; act as if you did.

C. S. Lewis, *Mere Christianity*

Week 28

July 9th – 15th

July 9th – 1958, C. S. Lewis published 'Revival or Decay?' in *Punch.*
July 10th – 1960, Warren Lewis read *Little Lord Fauntleroy* for the first time and agreed with C. S. Lewis that ridicule of the book must be caused by its sentimental illustrations.
July 11th – 1964, Warren Lewis dreamed that his brother C. S. Lewis came to him and asked for his prayer book.
July 12th – 1910, C. S. Lewis felt that he was moving into a life of bliss when he was released from his nightmarish boarding school in Malvern. The escape was a dream come true.

The world . . . is the beautiful frontispiece to Eternity.

One of the quotations from Thomas Traherne's*Centuries of Meditations* that Lewis sent to Greeves on July 8th

Week 29

July 16th~22nd

July 17th ~ 1930, C. S. Lewis warned his friend Arthur Greeves that beginning on this day he would be working on examinations from morning to night for about ten days.
July 21st ~ 1940, C. S. Lewis got his idea for writing *The Screwtape Letters* during a Sunday church service.

The next hour, the next moment, is as much beyond our grasp and as much in God's care, as that a hundred years away.

George MacDonald, 'The Causes of Spiritual Stupidity'

Week 30

July 23rd–29th

July 24th - 1921, C. S. Lewis' father visited him for the first time in the five years that Lewis had been at Oxford.
July 28th - 1944, C. S. Lewis published his poem 'A Dream' in the *Spectator.*
July 29th - 1913, C. S. Lewis published his first poem, '*Quam Bene Saturno*', in the Cherbourg School magazine when he was 14 years old.

C.S. Lewis in his study at Magdalen College, 1947. c Arthur Strong.

Merton College is one of the original three Oxford colleges, and dates back to 1264.

The 'New Buildings' at Magdalen College, dating from 1733,
seen from the deer park.

St Edmund Hall, smothered in wusteria, and the Front Quad.

Canterbury College Quad: upon completion, King Charles was received lavishly here: entertaining him cost as much as building the college.

Magdalen Bell Tower, with the frozen river Cherwell
in the foreground.

Magdalen College can be guessed at from the river Cherwell
in the late autumn.

Clive Staples Lewis in his rooms at Magdalen College.

For eating and reading are two pleasures that combine admirably.

C. S. Lewis, *Surprised by Joy*

Week 31

July 30th-August 5th

July 31st - 1944, J. R. R. Tolkein wrote to his son Christopher that he thought the hero of C. S. Lewis's first two science fiction novels was a portrait of himself.
August 2nd - 1928, C. S. Lewis wrote to Warren Lewis praising the writing of Samuel Johnson.
August 3rd - 1933, Warren and C. S. Lewis went on holiday to Scotland.
August 4th - 1922, C. S. Lewis received first class honours in Greats (Classics and Philosophy).
August 5th - 1922, C. S. Lewis received his BA. Warren Lewis was present for the occasion.

The brothers looked very much alike, and the sight of the two egg-shaped figures striding briskly along in animated conversation used to provoke amused comments . . .

Charles Wrong, 'A Chance Meeting', *C. S. Lewis at the Breakfast Table*

Week 32

AUGUST 6TH- 12TH

August 6th - 1941, on Queen Elizabeth, the Queen Mother's 41st birthday, C. S. Lewis gave the first of his 25 morale-boosting wartime talks on BBC Radio, later published as *Mere Christianity.*
August 7th - Eustace Scrubb, a character in C. S. Lewis's third Chronicle of Narnia, began keeping a diary on board *The Dawn Treader.*
August 8th - 1933, Warren and C. S. Lewis visited St Mark's Church in Belfast to see the stained-glass window they had placed there in memory of their parents.
August 11th - 1948, C. S. Lewis's poem 'The Late Passenger' was published in *Punch.* It told the story of the unicorn being left off Noah's ark.
August 12th - 1973, Charles Colson, aide to President Nixon, received C. S. Lewis's *Mere Christianity.*

C. S. Lewis's writings provided the sails required to begin my voyage to the new world of power and purpose available through the revealing love of Jesus Christ.

Charles Colson, on the BBC Radio programme, *I Call it Joy: C. S. Lewis Remembered*

Week 33

August 13th-19th

August 13th - 1948, Warren and C. S. Lewis saw Walt Disney's *Bambi* and rather liked it.
August 15th - 1932, C. S. Lewis began writing *The Pilgrim's Regress.*
August 17th - 1931, Warren and C. S. Lewis went bathing at Castlerock in Northern Ireland, scene of several childhood holidays.

A Christian is not a man who never goes wrong, but a man who is enabled to repent and pick himself up and begin over again after each stumble.

C. S. Lewis, *Mere Christianity*

Week 34

August 20th–26th

August 20th ~ 1958, C. S. Lewis completed his recording of *The Four Loves* for radio.
August 21st ~ 1934, Warren and C. S. Lewis were on holiday in Ireland and Warren went into an ocean made rough by wind and rain; he said it was the best 'bathe' he had ever had.
August 22nd ~ 1946, Warren and C. S. Lewis spent this evening with J. R. R. and Christopher Tolkien. C. S. Lewis read aloud his new poem about gnomes based on an idea from Paracelsus.
August 24th ~ 1957, C. S. Lewis wrote of his love for his wife, Joy, in a letter to his ex-student and friend Dom Bede Griffiths, a Benedictine monk in India.
August 26th ~ 1939, C. S. Lewis, Hugo Dyson and R. E. Havard left for a trip up the Thames on Warren Lewis's cabin cruiser, the *Bosphorus*.

Francis Thompson symbolised God as the 'hound of Heaven', pursuing on relentless feet. With me God was more like a cat.

Joy Davidman Lewis, 'The Longest Way Round'
in *These Found the Way*

Week 35

August 27th~ September 2nd

August 27th ~ 1939, as the Bosphorus moved upstream, a friend of C. S. Lewis canoed down the Thames past it, bearded and stripped to the waist – an unusual sight in those days.
August 29th ~ 1894, Warren and C. S. Lewis's parents, Albert and Flora, were married on this day.
September 2nd ~ 1939, children evacuated from London because of the bombing were received by Warren and C. S. Lewis at their home.

Anything large enough for a wish to light upon, is large enough to hang a prayer upon.

George MacDonald, 'The Words of Jesus on Prayer'

Week 36

September 3rd~9th

September 3rd - 1918, C. S. Lewis's first book of poems, *Spirits in Bondage*, was accepted by Heinemann publishing company.
September 4th - 1950, Warren Lewis attended the wedding of beloved Lewis friend Jill Flewett to Clement Freud, grandson of Sigmund Freud.
September 5th - 1931, Warren and C. S. Lewis clipped undergrowth in their woods with shears and sickle.
September 8th - 1947, C. S. Lewis was featured on the cover of *Time* magazine.

There was a boy called Eustace Scrubb, and he almost deserved it.
C. S. Lewis, *The Voyage of the Dawn Treader*

Week 37

September 10th–16th

September 10th - 1956, C. S. Lewis's favourite book, *Till We Have Faces; A Myth Retold*, was published.
September 11th - 1951, C. S. Lewis completed the last of three short holidays in Crawfordsburn, Northern Ireland; he had greatly needed the rest.
September 12th - 1960, J. R. R. Tolkien wrote to his son Christopher about his personal disappointment in C. S. Lewis's new book, *Studies in Words.*
September 13th - 1933, Warren and C. S. Lewis, holidaying in Hampshire, went for a stroll in Upper Canterton Wood. This place seems to have been the model for the Wood Between the Worlds that C. S. Lewis described 20 years later in *The Magician's Nephew.*
September 14th - 1949, C. S. Lewis's poem 'The Adam Unparadised' was published in *Punch.*
September 15th - 1948, C. S. Lewis's poem 'The Landing' was published in *Punch.* It tells of a long, difficult, sacrificial voyage to the utter West.

Tolkien was right. Although I became a friend of Lewis, I never 'got to the bottom of him'.

George Sayer, Preface to *Jack: C. S. Lewis and his Time*

Week 38

September 17th–23rd

September 19th - 1955, C. S. Lewis published his autobiography, *Surprised by Joy.*
September 22nd - 1952, C. S. Lewis was awarded an honourary Doctorate of Literature by LaVal University in Quebec.
September 23rd - 1944, J. R. R. Tolkien wrote to his son Christopher that he, Charles Williams and both 'Lewises' had enjoyed a good meeting a few nights before.

Wild Kierkegaard, Williams and Lewis
Guided me back to belief.

W. H. Auden, 'A Thanksgiving'

Week 39

September 24th–30th

September 24th - 1967, Warren Lewis attended, for the first time, a Sunday service at a Congregational Church.

September 27th - 1916, C. S. Lewis wrote to his friend Arthur Greeves to say that he was reading Milton's long poem 'Comus', an absolute dream of delight, all magic and distressed ladies and haunted woods.

September 28th - 1931, C. S. Lewis accepted Christianity on his way to Whipsnade Zoo with Warren Lewis.

I was driven to Whipsnade one sunny morning. When we set out I did not believe that Jesus Christ was the Son of God, and when we reached the zoo I did.

C. S. Lewis, *Surprised by Joy*

Week 40

October 1st - 7th

October 1st - 1931, C. S. Lewis mentioned casually in a letter to his old friend Arthur Greeves that he had recently become a Christian.
October 2nd - 1937, C. S. Lewis reviewed *The Hobbit* anonymously in the *Times Literary Supplement.*
October 3rd - 1944, poet-adventurer Roy Campbell met for the first time J. R. R. Tolkien, Charles Williams and Warren and C. S. Lewis.
October 5th - 1931, Warren and C. S. Lewis took their second trip to Whipsnade Zoo. They were both delighted with a fat brown bear that sat up and saluted for buns.

I enjoyed the walk in gentle steady autumn rain, smoke curling up slowly from the cottages, and the patter of the rain on the still brown trees . . . the country is beautiful at all seasons of the year.

Warren Lewis's entry in his journal on October 7th, 1930

Week 41

October 8th~14th

October 9th ~ 1946, Warren Lewis sat next to poet Ruth Pitter at a lunch party that C. S. Lewis gave for friends.

October 11th ~ 1930, Warren helped C. S. Lewis move into The Kilns. When Warren retired, the two would live there together the rest of their lives.

October 12th ~ 1930, a Mrs Armitage came for afternoon tea and insisted C. S. Lewis take her out on the pond in the punt. As a beginner, Lewis kept them gyrating helplessly in the middle of the pond, and Mrs Armitage suddenly sat down in an inch of black slime on the bottom of the boat. She laughed as much as everyone else.

It is imperative on us to get rid of the tyranny of things . . . We must possess them; they must not possess us.

George MacDonald, 'The Hardness of the Way'

Week 42

OCTOBER 15TH–21ST

October 16th - 1962, C. S. Lewis gave a lecture on BBC Radio about John Bunyan's *Pilgrim's Progress.*
October 19th - 1930, Warren and C. S. Lewis spent the afternoon wheeling books in from the garage and unpacking and shelving them in their new home, The Kilns.

Everyone has noticed how hard it is to turn our thoughts to God when everything is going well for us. We 'have all we want' is a terrible saying when 'all' does not include God.

C. S. Lewis, *The Problem of Pain*

Week 43

October 22nd–October 28th

October 22nd - 1939, C. S. Lewis delivered his rousing sermon 'Learning in Wartime' at the Church of St Mary the Virgin in Oxford.
October 25th - 1928, C. S. Lewis's first published book review appeared in *Oxford Magazine*. He reviewed Evelyn Waugh's *Rossetti*.
October 26th - 1918, C. S. Lewis went to London to see Heineman, his first publisher.
October 27th - 1912, C. S. Lewis's father wrote to him to report a dream he had had about a comet. Lewis's father was excited because, to him, the dream meant that C. S. Lewis was going to become succesful and famous.

The fantasy of growing old, like the fantasy of growing up, was part of the ineffable sweetness . . . of existence, itself the lordliest fantasy of all.

Charles Williams, *'Et in Sempternum Pereant'*

Week 44

OCTOBER 29TH–NOVEMBER 4TH

October 29th - 1957, C. S. Lewis wrote to a young Californian woman that she was the first critic he knew of who realised the connection of all his books – scholarly, fantastic, theological. 'This wins really very high marks indeed.'

November 1st - 1948, C. S. Lewis's poem 'The Turn of the Tide' was published. It told how all the universe rejoiced when Christ was born.

November 3rd - 1947, C. S. Lewis gave his talk 'A First Glance at Sartres' at the Socratic Club.

When the church becomes an idol, a thing mysteriously holy and powerful in itself, then the goal of religion becomes getting people to church – no matter why they go or what they get out of it.

Joy Davidman Lewis, *Smoke on the Mountain*

Week 45

November 5th~11th

November 6th ~ 1944, C. S. Lewis read his essay 'Is Theology Poetry?' at the Socratic Club.

November 9th ~ 1973, a caricature of C. S. Lewis in armour, defender of the faith, appeared on the cover of *Christianity Today* magazine.

November 10th ~ 1944, C. S. Lewis published the first chapter of his serial novel 'Who Goes Home?' in a church paper called the *Guardian*. It ran, chapter by chapter, until mid-April, 1945. Later it was published as a book called *The Great Divorce*.

Readers are advised to remember that the devil is a liar.

C. S. Lewis, Preface to *The Screwtape Letters*

Week 46

NOVEMBER 12TH~18TH

November 14th ~ 1970, Warren Lewis received a note from Blackwell's Bookshop informing him that a book he had ordered in 1957 was now available if he still wanted it. He answered yes.
November 18th ~ 1956, C. S. Lewis's article 'Sometimes Fairy Stories May Best Say What's To be Said' appeared in the *New York Times Book Review.*

Old age has stolen upon me . . . I am older than I was both in winters and in learning.

A quotation from about 1200 that J. R. R. Tolkien cited true about himself on November 14th, 1968

Week 47

November 19th–25th

November 19th ~ 1941, C. S. Lewis wrote to Sister Penelope, an Anglican nun, about some curious aspects of the Christian life such as our need for each other's insight.
November 20th ~ 1963, C. S. Lewis met Kaye Webb of Puffin Books. She was arranging for the first paperback edition of the Narnia Chronicles.
November 22nd ~ 1931, C. S. Lewis wrote an especially rich and descriptive letter to his brother Warren in China, telling about his day-to-day life and his appreciation of William Cowper's letters about day-to-day life.
November 23rd ~ 1944, an especially lively Inklings meeting was attended by the Lewis brothers, J. R. R. Tolkien, Charles Williams, Owen Barfield and Humphrey Havard. They discussed a play by Barfield, some poetry, ghosts and the nature of hymns.
November 24th ~ 1955, C. S. Lewis gave his talk 'On Science Fiction' to the Cambridge University English Club.

The only significance of Life consists of helping to establish the kingdom of God; and this can only be done by means of the acknowledgement and profession of the truth by each one of us.

Leo Tolstoy, *The Kingdom of God*

Week 48

NOVEMBER 26TH~DECEMBER 2ND

November 26th ~ 1942, C. S. Lewis preached his sermon 'Miracles' at St Jude on the Hill Church, London.
November 27th ~ 1953, C. S. Lewis wrote a letter to an American woman in which he responded to her agreement with his ideas on prayer by citing Scripture to show her that they are the Bible's ideas on prayer.
November 29th ~ 1898, birthday of Clive Staples Lewis.
December 1st ~ 1956, C. S. Lewis published his essay 'Behind the Scenes' in *Time and Tide*. In the essay he probed one of the mysteries of the human mind and, as an aside, took a guess at why Freud has been so popular.

While we are at prayer, but not while we are reading a novel or solving a crossword puzzle, any trifle is enough to distract us.

C. S. Lewis, *Letters to Malcolm*

Week 49

December 3rd~9th

December 3rd ~ 1954, C. S. Lewis gave his last tutorial at Oxford. He was leaving to assume the Chair of Medieval and Renaissance Literature that had been created for him at Cambridge.
December 4th ~ 1916, C. S. Lewis visited Oxford for the first time, to sit a scholarship exam.
December 6th ~ 1914, to please his father, C. S. Lewis was confirmed in the Church of England. Belief would come much later.
December 9th ~ 1954, C. S. Lewis was given a farewell dinner at Magdalen College, Oxford, in honour of his impending transfer to Cambridge.

How do you make a day holy? By seeing that it is holy already; and behaving accordingly.

Joy Davidman Lewis, *Smoke on the Mountain*

Week 50

December 10th-16th

December 11th - 1945, Warren Lewis, C. S. Lewis and J. R. R. Tolkien began a quiet holiday in Fairford celebrating the end of World War II.
December 13th - 1962, C. S. Lewis's BBC lecture 'The Vision of John Bunyan' was published in the *Listener.*
December 14th - 1950, C. S. Lewis wrote his first letter to Sheldon Vanauken, later author of *A Severe Mercy.*

I preserved hardly any of my innumerable conversations with J (C. S. Lewis). If only I had known . . . I would have Boswellized him.

Warren Lewis, *Brothers and Friends*

Week 51

December 17th–23rd

December 21st - 1932, Warren Lewis retired from the army.
December 23rd - 1918, Warren Lewis arrived home on leave for Christmas.

Since it is only too obvious that we can withold ourselves, our wills and hearts, from God, we can, in that sense, also give them.

C. S. Lewis, *The Four Loves*

Week 52

DECEMBER 24TH~31ST

December 27th ~ 1918, C. S. Lewis arrived home at Little Lea in Belfast after being released from the army.
December 29th ~ 1962, C. S. Lewis wrote to an American girl and told her that at his age time doesn't go 'fast', but 'at space speed'.

The secret of your own heart you can never know; but you can know Him who knows its secret.

George MacDonald, *The Seaboard Parish*